Robins Facing South

Robins Facing South

poems

J. Andrew Rodriguez

2004 • Red Mountain Press • Seattle, Washington

Published by Red Mountain Press
P.O. Box 16241
Seattle, WA 98116-0241

Red Mountain Press website address: www.RedMountainPress.com

Library of Congress Control Number: 2004094265

ISBN 0-9755981-0-4
First edition

Author photograph by V. Gayle Gillit
Cover and book design by Nautilus Design, Tacoma, Washington

Printed in the United States of America on acid-free paper

For my parents,
Agapito T. Rodriguez, Jr. & María Salomé Rodriguez

Acknowledgements

I owe a great many people who, in the course of my life, have lent their support and encouragement to my writing endeavors. Impossible as it is to list them all I will try, beginning with those that saw promise in my abilities early in my writing career, and urged me on. I am grateful to Ann Green, Ray von Rosenberg, Walter Price, Dr. Casey Skvorc, Dr. Rebecca Kennedy, Charles Dunsire, Patricia Black-Bailey, Dr. Stephen Feldman, Glenn Pascall, Maureen Larson, Sylvia Quiñones Sierra, and my writing group of Julie Miller, Wayne Gress, and Mary Bauer. And of course, my wife Gayle, whose love, support, patience, and faith in me were indispensable to the completion of this book.

Contents

III

IV

I

Two Brides, Two Dead Brothers

They sit, side by kindred side,
silent in the cacophony of a crowded migrant laborers camp,
hands bashfully wrapped around the
pearl of life that grows within each one.

Two widows, with Mona Lisa smiles,
look embarrassed to be fifteen.
Or was it sixteen years old?
Alone, without their husbands,
brothers, who found love in the
apple orchards, or the asparagus fields, or
maybe interlaced among the ribbons of
grapevines in the Eastern Washington valleys.

I blink back the sorrow that wells like a
tincture of silver in the corners of my eyes.
The migrants watch me blink back the silver.

The brothers were gone.
Their brief presence on this
earth ended with
speed melting into metal,
metal colliding with fury,
fury surrendering to death,
unconditionally,
on a contested lane of asphalt,
broken stripe down the middle.

I blink back the tincture of silver.

Each bride is too young to know the dead,
too young to strap a baby to her back
and walk along the rows of the fertile fields
to chop, or trim, or dig, or pick tender
crops with small and fragile fingers.

The tincture of silver overflows the
banks of my resistance,
clouds the panorama of my eyes,
subdues the color of youth,
and transforms the stoic portrait into
black and white.
Now that they are aged,
the brides may properly
grieve for their dead.

Soon, they will be mothers.
Soon, they will press their lips soft
against the ears of newborn babies
and whisper a story of death,
a tale of the fathers-to-be.
Two husbands,
two brothers,
too young to be dead.

Asking

I suppose, like a mist slowly dissipating
with the climbing of the sun,
I have faded from your memory.

I don't blame you.
The mist is so very difficult to corral
or predict or reason with.
My own entreaties are not raw.
Rather, they are undernourished and
confounded as to why.
No sooner are they presented than they
begin to shrivel from embarrassment,
and I am seized with the urge to withdraw,
lest such supplications be received
as onerous, and marched to the marrow of your duty,
where they act, unwittingly, to collaborate with the
oppressive weight of the day.

Betting the Mississippi

Ten years have passed since we last talked.
How your shores have changed.
Marianne warned me the casinos had come.
The casinos had changed everything.

Frenzied lights from the jamboree burst into the night.
The beacons call to the curious, miles away.
They travel the expanded Mississippi highways to this corner of
Tunica County, transformed into a striped sea of asphalt,
poured over the land like floods spilling from your banks.
The asphalt is as foreign here as in the desert.
Someone gave Las Vegas the keys to the Delta,
and the western interlopers came and stayed.

Moored casinos, with their cathedral ceilings, float over the
simmering rage of your waters. The arks of amusement
attract the bored, the desperate, the young, the old, and the lonely.
Listen as the believers whisper *sweet Jesus* into the
hand-cupped dice; see how they tremble at the edge of the
roulette table.

They assemble in the middle of bible country for a
baptism of chance or an electronic exorcism.
Renewal is only a covered bridge away, offshore of course,
valet parking optional.

The gamblers converge by day and by night.
Their forefingers slam quarters into the polished coin slots
that claimed the innocence of the previous customer,
and the one before that. The casinos sent buses out on
welfare check days, Marianne said, and handed out five-dollar
beer coupons. But the takers only drank, and some who
stayed lucky drifted away, check intact. The buses
stopped coming, but so did the welfare checks.
Nobody bet on that.

What a shame they have done this to you.
What a God-awful shame.
They cobbled together the machinery of greed
and lashed it to your face like a wound that tries
to set sail, but never leaves.

Norman, Oklahoma

The scarlet leaves of October erupt around
a young man's dream that stutters, talks, and then
begins to sing within days of coming into town.
Out of tune, and out of step, but it does sing.
The harmony is elusive, but it takes root and
begins to rise into the sunset blaze of trees alien to my eyes.

Warning signs disguised as electric welcome mats pulsate
above the college-kid bars, beckoning newcomers inside.
Noxious clouds spiral in synchronicity from the tips of
cigarettes lit in the twilight days of serving liquor by the *wink*.
The smell of cheap whiskey and the veil of blue smoke hover
over the floors, over the blessed red earth of Oklahoma.

In this land of the long-shot miracle worker and the
televangelist marathon, there is no better place to groom
a savior already infatuated with the prospect of piety.

Striking up conversations at the baseball game,
I insult the turquoise-clad Garcias and Montoyas by speaking
to them in Spanish. How could I have known they were Indians?
They tell me that their ancestors, the ones who
survived the Spanish *conquista*, were given Spanish names
when missionary friars baptized them as children of a
crucified god.

The Indians are a familiar brown, baking obligingly under the
contemplative ire of a summer sun, wearing faces like the
vacant copper masks hanging in the galleries.
Even their faces had been stolen.

In the mornings, white men glide along the milky curvature
of the garbage trucks, jerking the cans of refuse up and
over the paint-stripped edges. I was raised in the barrio of a
Texas town. White men did not collect trash. But here, white
men performed dirty work they could have thrown
a Mexican's way. Somehow, they had overlooked each other.

I try to slip colorless through the back door of law school
among the scions that wear pinpointed shirts, pressed to
cardboard consistency. They walk two abreast down the
crimson corridors of learning, bestowing smiles of practiced
insincerity on the audacious intruders devoid of the requisite
bloodlines who stray clumsily onto the spoken-for seats of
regal lineage. These are the things that happen when you
leave the back door open.

It is the common folk of the red land who take my flailing arms
and guide me through the prairie protocols that invite
strangers, the unsightly, the vagrant souls bracing for a break
to approach the altar of abundance and take what is needed.
It is always there to give.

We barter and borrow dreams in
street-lamp lectures and parking-lot pontifications,
betting who will save the world the fastest.

I am grateful for the perpetual mercies of Norman, but
doubts prey on my ambition. I plead for indulgence in
St. Thomas More's chapel. A candle burns during the agony of
bargaining in bad faith with God, crafting promises I cannot keep,
confessing errors yet to be committed,
negotiating between daily consultations with obligation
or its self-appointed impostor.

Lord, if not a lawyer, make me a saint of sorts,
a warrior drawn from the simple offerings of the plains.
Forge my spirit with the fire in the autumn leaves.
Sculpt my shield from the iron of the prairie will.
Teach me to dance to the rhythms of the ancient drums
that accompany the songs of a splendid people
who give what is needed.
It is always there to give.
Teach me to always remember,
remember Norman.

Done Lawyering

What you say, what you say?
I got to go to jail now?

Jail's not for me to say, Jacob.
The judge has done his part, and
I have done my part, the best I could.

You can't let 'em take me.
I got my wife. I got my little babies,
three, and one on the way.

I have done the best I could, Jacob.
The best I could.
My lawyering for you is done.
You best go now,
and go with the Lord at your side, Jake.

My pockets are empty.
My stomach is empty,
and that of my babies.
You, you take care of them, y'hear.

I'll do the best I can, Jacob,
just like I have done for you.

Naming Ángel

The orbits of your eyes tell the story of a ghost.
Eyes that are robbed of life, but life stirs nearby.
A torturer's flesh grows inside your young body.
A month at the hands of interrogators, you were
condemned to a Sandinista jail,
accused of complicity with the enemy.
Your days and nights were filled with terror.
One tormentor, then another, and another,
descending methodically upon you.

What will you do, refugee?
Nine months of desolation, you wandered alone.
Trespassing through Guatemala, then Mexico,
barren bus stations for your bedrooms,
begging fare and a transient bite of food
from the other refugees who stared at the
mirror of horror etched across your face,
the hidden face of war.
They recognized you.

What will you do, refugee?
The heartbeat from a nightmare grows stronger each day.
With each step you go farther and farther away from home,
heading north to cross a shallow crowded river.
The death grip of fear is wrapped around your waist.
A cruel souvenir swims in your womb.
Nine months to remember, nine months to decide.

You stand in the shade, frozen in place outside the hospital
on a windless Chihuahua desert day.
You are a frail bronze figure, shoulders slightly slumped forward,
arms cradling a dark baby.
You wait for me, for the car ride,
standing vigil over your anonymous interloper,
an uninvited stranger born ignorant of his father's face.

I need a name for my baby,
who is my friend,
my only friend on this journey.
I need a name for my friend.
Will you find a name for him?

Ángel can be your baby's name.
Each time they speak the name
of a child of a torturer,
what you will remember is your angel,
your friend, who stayed with you
during your journey,
during your flight from a nightmare.

A Bridge Well Built

There is no trace of the road back, or a trail, a worn swath in
the grass. A tide of indifference has encroached on my memories,
a tide escaping serious notice, or growing apprehension.

The indifference was a marvel of inconsequence, too
confident for my own good. Neglected relations floated away
as if on a silent ship of estrangement.

The ache of absence deepens each passing fall.
It signals another year of weathered dismay.
The ache comes with jaded resignation and nostalgia.

It is the stubborn wound of separation.
It is the longing that sits idly at the corner
of the table where we live and take our nourishment.
It is a longing summoned by the words on a page,
fleeting emotions from a stranger's glance,
or a vivid apparition seized from an honest, transient voice.
All reminders of what was lost such a long time ago.

A bridge is in order, the swiftest way back.
A bridge well built, of courage well founded,
and of good intentions, faithfully gathered, but badly in arrears.
Humility is present like a love song, a trusted guide
that shows the way back to the road.

A bridge is in order, not for retreat or elaborate excuse,
but for spontaneous rejoicing.
It is a bridge built for reunion.

If, however, waiting at the other of the end of the bridge is
an embellished ghost of the past,
somewhat embarrassed by the circumstances of our encounter,
I will be no less grateful for the effort,
and for the chance to rekindle the spirit of an old friend.

The Demon in Madness

This indelicate demon drives a hard bargain.
It seeks a friendly venue, a warm reception.
Why does it seem to defy direction?

Behaving like a guarded secret, prematurely released,
with no idea of what to do with itself but ruminate
in the morning, through the day, and into the evening,
the demon goes in search of some deserted
setting of silence. But it is bewildered, inconsolable, and riotous.
It wrestles with imponderable doubt, as would
an oblate contemplating treason.

What is concrete, and what is mayhem?
What alliances will prove dispositive of the demon?
Restless, clawing at its restraints with growing authority,
the demon, with cool invective, assigns assassins when
the knights of normalcy approach,
trying desperately to restore order.

The demon catapults across a shrinking channel of reason,
seizes the helm of the pendulum of sanity, and
swings it with monstrous abandon.

What will come of this demented demon?
This is the madness of mockery, of a revivalist torn
between duty and desire,
of a charlatan's insatiable lust for glory.
It is an aging sorcerer's impotent castigations,
of zenith imagined and zenith denied.
It is the quake of quiet compulsion to inflict injury,
so long as it is injury to self.

Robins Facing South

Two robins land on a tree after strumming the late winter
air to reach the top of the tree's twin masts. The burnt orange
of their breasts glows brightly against the waning shafts of
light from the setting sun. For a moment,
their prerogative is balance,
as the wind taunts the branches of the tree,
threatening a storm. But the wind is bluffing;
there will be no storm today.

The robins face south, without song, as if
anticipating a well-traveled visitor.
Maybe a youngster was overdue. Perhaps it
had turned away in mid-flight, without warning,
and without bidding farewell, knowing the time had
come to begin journeys of its own.

As the robins face south, I remember
those who were left behind when I began journeys
of my own. How they have aged. Their movements have
slowed with the passing years, the passing decades.
They stoop slightly. Their eyes are clouded and their
aches are pronounced. But I can only imagine them,
day by day, thousands of miles away. I think of birthdays missed,
milestones celebrated by proxy. My journeys take me
away from children who grow into men and women
faster than my sentimentality will accept.

The robins scan the southern horizon, and I think of
journeys I have made. There have been journeys of adventure,
of heartache, and even gross miscalculation.
The lessons have been harsh, and they have been sweet,
but I still search for the clarity of what has come to pass.

This much I know—the journeys would not be denied.
It didn't matter why. It didn't matter when. But destiny
wears a million masks, and it is hard to find the face of your
future without turning to take a close look. And what roads
lead to it you must follow.

I must follow, even when the journey leads home,
when those left behind bid a final farewell. The dreaded
afternoons will come, and I will wait my turn to sprinkle a
handful of freshly-dug earth over an open grave.
It is the journey that weighs the most, before and after.
It is a journey that will not be denied.

The robins face south, mindful of the advancing night.
First one, and then, with some hesitation,
the other, the robins leave their temporary stations
and drift further south, but not far,
as if to take a closer look,
before turning and flying back into
the ancient cycle of life.

Eulogy for an Artist

Today, we suffer the exuberance of a gallant dawn,
on the day we gather to mourn. I come to
a small Western Washington town to speak of a good friend.
This day we say farewell to an artist, whose
first canvas was the soil on the farm fields
he worked as a migrant.

I rise to speak, and take my place near the altar—something
I haven't done since high school, when I read epistles at
Mass because some people said I had a nice voice.
I believed them.

I look out at the faces that stare at me, and
all I see are breaking hearts. In my best epistle voice, I tell
them about Jesús Guillén. I tell them how he spoke
to us through canvas and paint and brush, charcoal and wood,
elements of the earth he so loved.

He painted the stories of brown-skinned people
who worked in the farm fields.
He was one of them. Jesús committed the color of their skin
to the eternity of the canvas.
When Jesús looked upon the fields of tulips and
daffodils, he saw a tundra of despair. And he painted it.
I tell them this was a man who saw genius in
everyone, and everything, and believed in the richness
of life. What a merciful God, I say, to have granted us a
chance to visit with him. But I don't remember reading
epistles of God's mercy.

I ask them to remember this gentle man,
this humble man, this loving man,
in the light of dawn,
in the dance of a field of daffodils,
in the glow of a harvest moon.

Remember him, I ask, when you look into the face of a
child, or hear the laughter of a friend. Remember him when
you stroll by a garden and smell the first gifts of spring.
And like the tulips he loved so much, when they have
shed their last remnants of glory, say of him, like them,
until we meet again my friend,
until we meet again.

"I don't cry," a social worker says, "and you made me cry."
"I don't cry," Dante, the youngest child says, "but you
made me cry."
"You're a pretty good poet," a stranger says, "for a lawyer."

Or am I? I feel Don Jesús put his arm around me,
grin, and say "Amigo, enjoy the compliments, please, I insist."
I see the words drawn on his golden, thin tracing paper,
the kind he used for his letters,
words sketched by the wings of my imagination.

I thank you, my friend. And I don't cry either.

Anita's Dream

Under a quilted blanket of broken clouds,
she waits. Beneath the bursting blossoms of her cherry tree
that drift like kite tails orphaned by the tantrum of an
early-morning gale, she sits, silent on the wooden bench,
saving the worn space next to her,
and waits for the man of her dreams to come back.

She says she's just a plain old woman.

She waits patiently for the rituals of spring, and
spring's children that rise in homage to her.
They rise through the nourished earth, the anointed
ground that she has cultivated as her garden.

They obey her, the plain old woman,
who surely cups sunlight in the palms of her hands,
mixes streams of leftover sky into the soil,
then sprinkles low-hanging stars at night,
when no one is watching.

She says she is a plain old woman, who looks across the
veranda and sees the padlocked hut with its empty easel,
wrinkled paint tubes, and stationary oil brushes that ache
for the fingers of a master.

The plain old woman remembers the man in her dreams
as she sits beneath the stoic stare of the farm workers he painted.
The brown mother, the brown father, and the brown children,
their yellow-gloved hands clutching and hauling the
rapturous bundles of freshly-cut daffodils and tulips
in the muddy Skagit Valley fields.
The man who lives in her dreams painted them
stooping and chopping, and chopping and stooping
all day, as he once did.

She dreamed, quietly, as he slipped away,
through the slim crack in the wall of his defiance,
slipped through the outstretched arms of his beloved *vieja*,
past the rocky monuments he left in the garden.
He slipped in and out again of the shuttered artist studio
one more time. Just as his last, magnificent act of art came to life,
he died.

A plain old woman,
plain as the sun,
plain as the sky,
plain as the bursting blossoms of a cherry tree,
waits, and remembers the man in her dreams.

II

Grave Digger for a Mexican Baby

"Deeper, no, deeper still,"
the white, sunglassed city clerk says in an accent
thick with a homegrown Texas drawl.
Her horsewhip voice cracks downward
through her pursed, fire-engine-red lips
into the rectangular hole in the earth.
These are stifling words almost as heavy as the
late morning coastal air of another
brutal cloudless August day.
She is annoyed at her fate this day.

The clerk lady wants a grave,
a baby's grave.
I swing the pickax hard into the blackened southern
soil that bites fiercely into the iron blade of the instrument
and tries to swallow it and me whole.

With every thrust of my upper body, I arm-wrestle
the earth for a pound cake's worth of its flesh.
Down and up and out.
Down and up and out.
The attack and counter-attack are relentless, but dignified,
as we are at a cemetery.
When the sweat pores flood the torso and
blind my eyes with stinging salt,
another Mexican jumps in for his turn.

It is an impromptu grave
for a Mexican baby, on the Mexican side of the cemetery,
on the Mexican side of the railroad tracks.
Choked to death on a weenie, the clerk lady tells us,
in the chaos after the hurricane that paralyzed our
two-stop-light town with its new Dairy Queen, and its
new Mexican baby boy.

"No," the Anglo lady says, "that's just not deep enough.
Give me six feet Red Cross boys.
Keep digging."
She has no tractor or water for us today.
She just needs a grave for a dead Mexican baby.

"Hurry up."

Road Trip to College

Sunday, he slips me a 20 before I climb into my
'71 Plymouth Duster, headed back to Austin.
How many haircuts did this take?
How many stories did he hear from the customers who
came from the cotton gin, or the Reynolds plant,
or the filling stations, or the farms?
The men who came to him because he was a good man,
and a good barber, the men who called him out Saturday
nights after he came home because they needed to look
sharp for the dance, and only a fresh haircut would do
for a dance.
How many hours standing behind that barber chair?
The 20-dollar bill weighs a ton in my hand.
I know how much it cost him.

I can't, I tell Dad.
"Sure, keep it, no problem," he says.
"Wish I could give you more, I really do."
It's all right, I tell him. It will keep me warm,
just like those freshly-made tortillas mamá
tightly wrapped in aluminum foil,
tortillas soon to be laid one after the other
on the dashboard defroster, on the road to college,
and eaten with gratitude.

"Wish I had more, son, wish I did.
You let me know if you need more.
I don't want you hurting for a hamburger."

Father's Day

From behind a rumpled, gauze-colored hospital gown,
he awakens. Tubes descend unceremoniously from above his bed.
They wrestle for space with the wires that sense for
signs of life and hoped-for resurgence of a temperamental heart.
So many tubes affixed to so many places, he almost
dangles like a puppet. Sleep is shattered by the convulsions
of an enraged chest, sliced nearly in two for the sake of
repairing his damaged heart.

He wakes to a symphony of beeps and squawks, incessant
humming, an annoying honk. Banks of monitors,
like applause signs, blink green, red, amber, and white with the
synchronicity of harbor buoys, surging, then falling,
like the swells of an approaching storm.

Wake up, open your eyes!
Today is Father's Day.
HAPPY FATHER'S DAY—You're getting a hearing aid.
Can you hear us?

An extra sip of water, a blanket over exposed toes are
extra gifts. A freshly-soaked towel is laid on a sweaty forehead.
A father's spirit lives in the hearts of his children,
an African proverb says in a greeting card.
Greeting card.
Will he remember?
No, nothing, because of the thick, milky amnesiac that slithers
behind him from an upside-down bottle and drains into a plastic
port fused to a central line.
No, he will not remember.

After a half-doughnut's celebration, we must go, but
not before the Eucharistic minister slips in quietly, like the
thin wafer delivered bedside to his eager mouth.

It is time to fade to sleep, sleep and rest, and cough and sleep.
And the lights above pulsate green, red, amber, and white,
like buoys on the cusp of an approaching storm.

Blind Man News

What Edwin Newman never knew was that he was blind.
Not that it bothered him, or served as an impediment to his
job as a newsman on NBC-TV.
To a five-year-old, Edwin Newman did just fine.

He read the noontime news admirably well, through empty eyes,
white papers propped up in his hands,
effortlessly glancing up, then down, again and again,
speaking clear, relaxed words about stories that must have
been very important.
His face said so.
And the Mexican music floating over from the kitchen
didn't seem to bother either one of us,
but only I could smell the crushed cumin seeds.

That's what my eyes could see: a gray man, in a gray suit,
with a gray tie, but with no eyes, only gray circles within
white globes on either side of his nose.
Funny thing that a tiny rabbit-eared black-and-white TV would
bring us news from the blind but not about the blind
(as far as I could tell).

Nobody told me that color TV could give
a person blue eyes.

Why would anybody want blue eyes anyway?

Camarada's Cosmos

Who took him from us we will never know.
Surely someone bored to the brink of a coma,
or maybe a bureaucrat who let the monthly quota of
involuntary commitments slip behind schedule,
and became alarmed.
But somebody had called the sanity police and
they set out to find their man.

Lanky and gray-haired, Camarada sported a Ho Chi Minh
set of whiskers. He regaled us with stories of his latest imaginary
trips to Japan, lighting his cigarette at the wrong end,
distracted by the intensity of his own conversation
as he ate his customary half bowl of chili at the Taco Hut.

Faded cane at his side,
his dog faithfully outside the door,
the comical man in the ragged vest and tattered coat was
immune to the puzzled stares of his appreciative audience.
Camarada captured the fascination of all his invented
compatriots and all of us laughed in joyous celebration of
each other's company.

But someone took him away from us.
Someone careless had him snatched in the middle of a story,
and they took him to San Antonio.
We all knew what that meant—the crazy house.
They incinerated his brain to cure him of it,
and hollowed the cosmos out of his head.

Their mission accomplished, the sanity police deposited
Camarada in the barrio where they had found him.
They took a gentle man away from us and
brought back a zombie in a macabre malaise,
an alien to laughter.

He was back, but Camarada was gone.
And so were his stories.
The shell of a man drifted away
in pursuit of an echo of his laughter.

Someone took Camarada away from us one day.
Maybe they were scared of his laughter.
Maybe they were afraid to laugh.

Missionary Daughters

The lunch was set before my brother and me,
each with a neatly arranged white-bread sandwich,
the crust meticulously trimmed away.
The white cube was thinly cut along a diagonal line.
Two slices of thin bread encasing a glistening brown
layer of refried beans served in the modest parlor of the
convent opposite the semi-retired wooden church still
able to host dances and house the belfry.

The kind meal came from the
Missionary Daughters of the Most Pure Virgin Mary.
Teachers from a Mexican order, they were
sent to save souls and teach Christ to Mexican people
in *Norteamérica*.

The Brides of the Church learned baseball, and pitched
during recess. Sister Jovita stepped up to the pitcher's
mound once and got knocked in the forehead by my
cousin's line drive. Forgiveness was a team sport.
What good sports they were as they strained
to explain, in English, the milk-bottles diagrams
in the catechism book, venial versus mortal sins
painted as black watermelon seeds.
Could they explain the seeds one more time, please?

The dreaded day came,
the day they knew about, but hoped would not arrive.
The new priest, the German, tall as a palm tree,
saw no money on the books. No money, no school, no sisters.
And they were gone,
unemployed missionary nuns looking for a job.
Did we ever understand what they meant to us?

Their love was the soul of the barrio. There was soul in that
faded yellow-brick schoolhouse, with the varnished fir floors
and the eternal hallway to the Mother Superior's classroom.
One solo stroll there was evidence enough of eternity.

The missionary daughters climbed into their station wagon
and drove away from a barrio that turned and shrugged.
No protest rallies, no denunciations of everything German,
no last-minute pledge drives.

The vacant schoolhouse became a mausoleum of memories,
a lonely shrine, a Head Start program.
But never again was it a schoolhouse filled with the sisters
who sliced bean sandwiches for two hungry brothers,
who pitched the love of Jesus and the merits of mercy
to the forsaken children of a forsaken Texas barrio
that let its only salvation slip away in a station wagon,
a station wagon full of brides.

The Mayor's Son's Shirts

What splendid cloths they are:
fine linen for the oppressive subtropical air,
button-down collars, tight stitching in perfect single-file
formation up and down the crisp short sleeves.
The colors dazzle in patterns designed
to be proudly worn by a mayor's son.
And so they were, until cast aside and found by
the mayor's housekeeper, who lived down the street from us.

"Look at these," the mayor's housekeeper says to my mother,
eyebrows raised as she unfolded the limp orphans
taken from a closet more regal than the one I shared with
three others.
"I'll take them," mamá says to the housekeeper.
"How much?"

Jubilant, my mother presents the prizes to me.
"Look at this one, this other, and how about this shirt?"
Rotten is too sweet a word for the luck I feel.
My two school-year shirts are not ungrateful for the company,
yet I fear the collection of fibers on my back
will announce a mayor's son's shirt in a school hallway
like a political convention on its feet for the
nominee's acceptance speech, party hats and all.

There are ninety-nine students in my class, plus ninety-nine
juniors, and maybe one hundred seniors. In this small high school,
there are not enough ruffles, or plaids, stripes, or checks
to camouflage my recent acquisitions. Never enough
bell-bottoms, paisley print, or tie-dyed T-shirts, or
disco polyester, or—

"Hey, nice shirt," the mayor's son says to me, grinning through
his silver-wire teeth.

Why thank you, I say.
Thank you…very…much.
Would you like a party hat?

III

Forgiveness and I

I am a perpetual penitent,
the eternal student of remorse,
practicing the act of self-forgiveness.
One forgiving another is a gift to both.
Forgiving self, however, is an elusive endeavor,
an art perhaps best reserved for mystics.

From time to time I sail
the channels of regret, and
steer through an archipelago of imperfections,
real and imagined. The waters of regret run wild.
They are like rapids that agitate with the
anguish of old unpardoned errors.
I seek consultations with regret, but it is like a dissident
ambassador who will not come home.

I have made a study of omissions, the times when
not enough was said and not enough was done.
Keeping company with omissions makes for long
and tortuous nights. In some way, we all carry a journal
of remorse. In the pages are words of wounds, and
wounds of silence.

In between revisions of my past, small victories of
forgiveness emerge through the cracks in the
granite of my guilt. I salute the small victories,
and I embrace them when I make peace with my regrets and
seek pardon of myself.

I am who I chose to forgive.

True forgiveness, kind in its reverence for the
transparency of a fool,
cleanses the nucleus of the soul,
ordains transformation,
and with a crude club
chases the inevitable rats of revision
down a blind alley,
where they belong.

Celebration

To celebrate the elegance of life, entertain the following:

Sliding across a prism's blade of light
Floating down a mandolin's string of laughter
Capturing, then releasing, a love sonnet's dove
Pinching a sweet dream gently to make sure you're asleep
Sipping on a freshly-served tonic of contentment,
squeeze of lemon, please
Planting a tree of remembrance in the garden of your youth
Tumbling jubilant into the astonishment of rediscovery
Partnering with courage to steal a glance at forbidden desire
Taking a meteor shower with a long-lost love
Singing duet with an early-morning rainfall
Skipping rocks across a reservoir of unneeded tears
Painting pastels in a baptistery for prodigal illusions
And don't forget
Coaxing a lighting bolt from a pregnant purple cloud to
jitterbug across the sky

Wren Rising

I heard the Bewick's wren singing again today,
exercising its usual unerring a cappella splendor,
bellowing beauty with every flush of its lungs,
perched princely on a narrow telephone line,
calling out to the west, proclaiming its incontestable
reign over some small dominion.
Long may it live.

So I saved the songs for you
in the sanctuary of the garden.
I tucked a melody behind the skyward spiraling jasmine.
Pluck a vine to release it.

Folded into the crowded petals of a dripping English rose,
there is an octave as high as the tip of the ancient cedar tree.
A song vibrates the bloom with the vigor of a summer's
afternoon breeze.
Smell the rose to listen.

In the blackberry lily you will find an aria.
Gently caress the unsuspecting spotted petals with the
elegance of your fingers, and you will release the
accompaniment to the vespers of angels.

Linger and listen
to the triumph of sound,
to the celebration of song,
and the unconditional embrace of the joy of the day.

All there, waiting for you when you return
the day after tomorrow.
Gifts sent to you by the darting rising-tailed wren,
who may yet greet you with harmony and an encore.

Uncle Everett's Joy

An uncle's arms, thin like autumn twigs
bracing for Kentucky's winter's edge,
float upward after releasing the yellowed cane.
Tears fill his still adolescent eyes.
His voice and arms tremble with excitement.
A boy, 52 years young, has arrived, and
says hello to an old man.

Come,
give me a hug, David.

Riddle of the Word

We neglect the intentions of our words.
They escape clear inspection,
float in the dead space of conversation,
then go through unrehearsed motions of
intelligent assessment, wondrous insight, or
unbelieving fascination, sometimes all in
the same breath.

The words are innocent enough.
We mean well, but we are not scientists.
We forget the alchemy of our words and,
sometimes by accident, we create wild notions that
if left untamed, fan the flames of idle chatter.

There are reasons we speak in riddles,
but they are not always clear.
The time for careful deliberation of what we want to say
shrinks more every day. Still, we can try to stamp our words
with delicacy and precision.

Even so, sometimes the riddle of the word haunts us.
Haunting is not the sole province of the dead;
the living can participate just as well
simply by opening their mouths.

We are not scientists, and though we are not skilled sculptors,
we chisel our words and try to free them from false foundations.
The stones of our words are often cumbersome, heavy, and
encrusted with miserable shards. Others are smooth and polished,
perfect for spontaneous eating.

But it is from these gems, unparalleled, undisciplined, and
some even unruly in each other's company,
that we take our comfort and learn to practice our tenderness,
if we try.

Obligation

On awakening again,
with half the twilight from the morning
already gone, I cling to you.
You, utterly consumed by me,
by my ill-placed contentment seeking
a transient respite, a safe harbor.
We lie cheek next to irreverent cheek in complete silence,
careful to avoid the negligence of sincerity.
I roll away, clutching at the watery-thin membrane
of a recurrent stillborn dream of rekindled youth.
Maybe a returning favor, long since given up as lost,
will bring a fresh prospect today. Fresh prospects feed
my stream of restlessness.
An obliging squeeze, not without tenderness, then I am gone.
A key's turn separates me from one more moment of affirmation,
but a lingering glance convinces me to walk.
The echo of retreating footsteps
fades like a nostalgic song,
like the ascending ash of a
once undaunted fire.

The Search for a Lost Soul

A shaman told me where to find you.
The last one you saw told me to follow the trail of
the gangrene of greed and to look for the
scoliosis of the will.
The ganglia of suspicion formed in your early adolescence,
and has spread beyond its original boundaries.
A collapse of resolve is evident in second guesses that are
scattered over the years, in all directions.
Then there is the fourth consecutive attempt at religion,
overshadowed by nostalgia for the early Pentecostal years.
A crucible of courage smolders in its own ashes.
It is an early fire, poorly contained and fueled by a
well of avoidance.
The oil of redemption stained your soul,
but there is no trace of redemption, not that I can see.
Your rendezvous with catharsis failed; you were a no-show.
You beached integrity on an island only you can find,
when you are sober enough to read the map.
Pride and arrogance are your sentries and they
wear the confidence of sustained success.
The embrace of recklessness is behind you, but the
jackal of madness nips at your heels.
Where once a pessimist's myopia crippled you,
it is indifference that now blinds you.
So the shaman wishes to lend you his eyes.
But take mine instead, if you promise to give them
back when you have found your way.

Some Other Day

Idleness sucks the vigor out of life.
Maybe that is why I feel so tired. I think
of cross-country skiing, and I get the chills.
I can kayak in the Puget Sound, but I could also
turn over, which would make me the rough
equivalent of a cork in an upside bottle of merlot,
except that I would be drowning. I might run in
a marathon, but I'd have to sit some place
comfortable and think about it first.

When life comes full circle, as it must, I hope
it is not on a day burdened with monotonous
distractions and pathetic excuses shouting over one another.
When the final, defining call comes,
the summons of dread will find me gone. I want an escape route,
a pre-rehearsed excuse why I will not be available.
I could ski and kayak and run, all on the same day.
I could.

Some other day would be more fitting.
Some other candidate is preferable, someone in better shape,
who is at once transformed and transforming.
Someone who possesses unflinching courage and boasts
abundant resolve is more suitable. Perhaps a baseless braggart
would do, maybe one who eluded his own day of reckoning
and now, emboldened, taunts his returning avenger.
In other words, not me.

This unpretentious soul, innocuous by design, gladly yields
his number to someone else. There are no disingenuous
ambitions here, no alliances with tricksters, no lustful grasp
on a rein of power.

No, all I present is a plea, from one as pretentious as a flea,
for another day's grateful chance to scratch out the sweetness
of life.

A Gospel Mission Beating

Gloom roams the streets like a gang this autumn morning.
The sun sent a surrogate that got lost along the way.
Restless clouds, seizing the opportunity, hang low and
spit like gargoyles furloughed for the day.

I walk past a black man.
Bulging garbage bags trail him like a pack of curious dogs,
the possessions of his life rotting at the end of a plastic knot.
Food is on his mind, hunger on his face.

What concern to me?
Another homeless man stopped to knock at a gospel mission,
where Jesus and a free meal can save you,
one forever, the other for the time being.

"Go away," the two white men inside shout through the glass.
The man continues to knock, and tap, and even pound.

"We don't open until this afternoon, come back then!"

He is mechanical with his knocking.
Who wound him up and set him on the street?

Knocking
      Knocking
         Knocking

Suddenly, a commotion; glass doors are kicked violently open.
I turn to see the two white men mauling the black man.
One holds the black man from behind, the other pummels him
with both fists. The black man, resigned to his reception,
puts up weak resistance.

He falls, hard, kissing the street with the bones of his cheeks.
There was no talking, there was no preaching.
In an instant it is over, and the man with the plastic bags flees.

It could not have been hard for them to beat a poor man
that day. Rage poured from the vessels of salvation into a man
who forgot the velocity of pain, who forgot
the gospel of the streets.

Pedestrians, preemptively inoculated, witness the brutality,
but no one broke stride.

They will not rescue a man this October morning.
Neither will I, not while wearing a pin-striped suit,
a crisp white shirt, and Johnston & Murphy loafers,
tassels smart and intact.

Humanity collapsed before my eyes. Humanity slumped
against the pinstripes that became the bars to my cell.
The mission, on this miserable autumn day, had changed,
but only for a moment that, like a dime, no one could spare.

Breathless at the Border

My fists rock methodically, like pistons, as I
run through the unattended gate.
I exploit the incompetence of a border guard, and
leap across a cartoon river,
traced along the western spur of Texas.

Looking backwards as I run,
I stumble over desert rocks.
I suck hot dust down my trachea.
I race through the commercially zoned,
urine-soaked alleys of a border town.
The convulsive fumes corkscrew into my nostrils.

I have been here before,
and searched along the river's edge for the love of God,
but only found the skulls of my brothers, my cousins,
my predecessors.
Hermano, is that you?
The *coyotes* celebrate today, as usual,
counting tainted cash raised from charging their human cargo
the market price of chance, adjusted for despair.

Like a hundred sheep, a million, headed north,
we, the festering hordes of discarded humanity,
lean eagerly, throat-first, into the thin barbarous line that
separates us from the promised land.
My goddam promised land.

A blue-eyed *pistolero*, gun in hand, picks up my trail.
Overhead, the air pulsates with the rhythm of chopping blades.
He hunts with his helicopter.
It darts impatiently, like a mechanical dragonfly.
The gold of the pistolero's badge, shiny against
a deep green uniform, matches the rims around my rotting teeth.
The pistolero, careless, runs past my crouched shadow.
He orders the dragonfly to dive and seize his quarry.
It fails, this time.

I hold my breath and pray for the refuge of a sewer ditch,
maybe the rolling inferno of a boxcar. My lungs ache and
I collapse to my knees behind an overflowing dumpster,
next to a jack-knifed, open-jawed body,
teeth set with dull, gold rims.

My hunter returns with another pistolero at his side,
gun drawn,
a crisp green uniform,
dark brown eyes,
and gold around the rims of his polished teeth,
like the shimmering surface of his newly-pinned badge.

A breathless man,
a dragonfly,
a new pistolero,
and a river, bled dry of hope.

The Patience of Kindness

For want of a generous syllable,
or a benign phrase,
even a gesture requiring no more forethought
than a passing but attentive glance,
a kindness goes unclaimed.

Wide-eyed with expectation,
dressed in Sunday's best,
preened, polished, sharp at attention, an act of
kindness anxiously stands in line next to the other brimming,
would-be adoptees waiting at the train stop,
at the grandstand of human conciliation.

Kindness conducts court among its fellows,
some disappearing into the mold of neglect,
stiff without being exercised regularly or with
sincere intent.

The gathered optimists, whipped by the wind of another
passing and missed opportunity,
shrug in unison, turn around, and begin to walk away,
but not before marking the very spot with the flag
of faith that soon they will be back
at the grandstand,
at the train stop where kindness waits in perpetuity,
but not in vain.

Contemplation

I listen to the whispers of once-heralded truths,
when regret posts its mail a day late,
when prayer pleads for mercy to stay out of a fight,
when vision boasts of its fake fidelity,
when promises mock the believers who have been deceived,
when heartache begs abuse for another chance,
when delusion offers to buy a round for the house,
when passion leads reason on a joy ride through dirty sheets,
when faith keeps company with a jilted saint,
when memory serves a warrant for a plea bargain secret,
when greed holds hostage the soul of a rising star,
when ambition takes civility out back for a beating,
when prudence forges a lottery ticket on a dare.

I walk barefoot,
to the marbled edge of my soul,
and listen
to the fading whispers of once-heralded truths.

Rare Wound

As prayers go, you are someone I am not supposed to have.
It doesn't keep me from praying, and the answer comes to me in
an apparition of an elixir, your special formula of estrangement.

But come to me anyway, and bring my delusion with you.
Consort with me and believe you are mine. Deliver to me
a rare wound, the kind that mimics euphoria, the kind
that seduces and betrays while it plots a dishonorable escape.

You are fleeting, unrepentant, and ruinous with your cares.
You are only passing through, but you minister to me
as you would a leper, a beggar in the rain, beset
by your scant affections. How you come to me, angelic yet cruel,
for the few hours that you can spare, the hours
that you salvage for me, like the faith you restore, and
then discard.

So long as you linger, let me stroke the phosphorescence of
your love in the darkened corners of my life, the ones
I curse by habit, the habit I curse when you exit with apology,
even though I expect none.

Bus Stop

Tonight, trapped by the miserable traffic congestion that
trapped my bus, I wait. I clutch my wool coat tightly
against the chill, at the bus stop,
1st and Jackson.

Just enough daylight loiters for me to break out my paperback
copy of *The Stranger* by Camus. The usual fugitives of the night
straggle along the sidewalks. Some bum change off the
shopkeepers and their customers. Others are unconscious,
their wilted bodies splayed across a rusted drainage grate.
The lucky ones are wrapped in a cocoon of cardboard.

A couple approaches, one of them chain-smoking.
One of the two was hardly more than a child,
the two clearly mother and daughter. As they draw close,
I notice their speech patterns are not clear.
Sounds are slurred, almost unintelligible.
They chatter, like parakeets, non-stop.
They cannot stand still.

Mother and daughter stroll to a nearby ledge
to sit out the bus wait, then back again to the curb,
and back once more to the ledge. A shabby man,
on one aluminum crutch, ambles around the corner shouting,
but at no one in particular. He decides to stand near me.

I squint harder at the pages, drawing in nearer as
natural light ebbs away. Suddenly, from the corner of my eye,
I see mother and daughter hop off the ledge
and stride toward me. Arriving at my left elbow,
they begin to speak.
I lower *The Stranger* and smile.

"You know what?" the daughter asks. "The Lord let me out of
the hospital today; yes He did, after three weeks."

"Good for you," the shabby man volunteers. "You're out."
He seems to understand something I do not.
"She had a nervous breakdown, she did," the mother offers.
"Why, I don't care what she had," the old man says.
"As long as she's out, looking to the future.
That's the good news."

The cigarette smoke the man blows,
and the stench of alcohol on his breath, deplete my patience.
I step away, but the girl hovers close by.
I turn to her.
"How old are you?"
"Sixteen," she proudly replies.

A pretty young girl, not yet a woman, she seems stuck
in her early childhood. Maybe mom is mentally retarded;
maybe they both are. It saddens me. And it sickens me that
a sixteen-year-old could be hospitalized for a nervous breakdown.

I edge back out to the street, craning my neck for any sign of
my bus, the 21 or the 22.
I seize on the vague outline of a bus, blocks away.
The mother suddenly reappears with a demand for my attention.
"Hey!" she says. "Is your name Andy?"

Pain
Gut
Pain

How in the hell could she have known that was my name?
What were the odds of her hitting on that one name alone?
I hesitate.

"Why do you ask that?"
"I just want to know if your name is Andy," she replies.
"That's all. Because you look just like somebody I used to know,
somebody named Andy."

"Where did you know this Andy, and when did you know him?"
"Oh, in Marysville or Lake Stevens, back in 1970.
Andy and his wife Sandy. Andy and Sandy."
"Yeah, Andy and Sandy," the daughter repeats, and giggles.
"They could have a baby and name it Candy."
"Well," I assure her, "I've never been to Lake Stevens, but I
hear it's beautiful country."

Just then a brightly lit bus, with the number 21 glowing on a
panel arrives, surely sent from heaven.
"Well," I say with some relief, "this is my bus."
I climb aboard, clutching *The Stranger* slightly tighter than usual.

I glance over my shoulder to see if they stayed on the curb.
"Sure hate to leave those girls out there before their bus shows
up," the aluminum crutch man says, ambling up behind me as
we board the bus.

But they are survivors.
I know it.
They know it too, even if it did take a psychiatric ward
to make them believe it.

As the bus pulls away, I look out the window at them
one last time. Only then do I realize that
I never told them my name.

Flight of a Terrorist

I am the unseen,
the inconsolable, the doubter, the doubted.
I am hatred incarnate.
I am unclean, unwashed, disheveled, and abused.
I am hungry, my gaping mouth unnoticed by the hurried
passerby.
I am spent of compassion.
I am angry.
I am scornful and bitter.
I am a liar, a disbeliever, a dispossessor of hope.
I am indigent, I am rich in misery.
I am impatient with He who created me, with He who
deserted me,
but who I dare not desert, who I serve with my blood.

I am discounted and disowned.
I am afraid.
I am ashamed.
I am besieged by the cries of wailing mothers.
I create wailing mothers.
I abhor the sound of truth.
I am the bastard of death.
I spit upon pity, yet I command it by the legions.
I am revolted by the face in the mirror,
yet I am faced with the revulsion of my ambition.

Spreading my righteous wings wide,
diving steeply through the air in the early hours of the morning,
I turn sharply and, with fixed aim,
I consecrate the orange fire of redemption,
and flash the grin of infinity.

Disgorging a Piñata

When I arrive in the valley, I remember the bougainvillea.
They rampage indiscriminately through all the neighborhoods,
rich and poor. The scarlet, lavender, and purple flowers
decorate a plain landscape lined with immigrant palm trees and
freshly upturned dirt from the vanishing orange groves.

I am sent to the courthouse, and I find the atmosphere like
that of a carnival. Well-dressed revelers converge as if waiting
for piñatas of greed to drop from balconies at the courthouse,
through black-robed curtains. The piñatas in the valley have
deep pockets, and the revelers are restless and anxious to beat
the piñatas senseless with their sticks.

After a school bus full of children is knocked into a canal,
a large crowd quickly gathers at the courthouse. They wait
for a piñata. Children are maimed; children are dead.
The crowd chants "justice, justice." A piñata is expected,
a piñata unlike any other.
There will be no blindfolds this time.

Finally, the piñata appears, spinning down from the balcony.
Excited, the revelers strike at it with their sticks. The piñata,
in the shape of some ghastly creature, teases the revelers.
They swing their sticks and beat the piñata, and each other.
One of the revelers yells to me: "Hang around kid, and you'll be a
millionaire in no time." Suddenly, the belly of the beast is
ripped open, and the spoils of tragedy tumble down upon
the crowd.

Out of the corner of my eye I notice a thin procession. I am
told that they are pariahs. They disdain the carnival and its
spinning piñatas of greed. They curse it all. The pariahs carry
no sticks. They find no welcome in this valley. They are
sickened by what they see, and frightened by the
scarcity of their numbers.

I look at the procession, then at the strange stick in my hand,
then again at the pariahs. They march in exodus and leave
the valley, under the arched blooms of the bougainvillea.
They turn for a final glance at the few, native pariahs who
choose to stay.

The pariahs are scarred, but they are not defeated.
Each carries a busted rosary in one hand, the black onyx
crucifix clinging tenuously to a mystery.

Where does one recycle such things?

Confession

The confession hangs in the air like the blade of a guillotine.
He thinks, idly, how easy it is to fail to learn from failure.
He has been here before.
If only it was because of youth, insatiable lust of youth.
But those years are distant enough to forget, or the memories
fell victim to neglect.

Besides, youth requires no apology, he thinks to himself.
He is brave, but not brave enough to feel repentant.
There is a sound to it all, an octave above a sigh.

They stare in silence away from each other and at the
gray corpse of trust. It lies motionless, beyond recognition,
as if it had succumbed to some savage disease, as if
waiting to be embalmed.

They sit on the bed, in the alien sanctuary of their room.
Although this is a confession, it is the sacrament of extreme
unction that is required, the last rites for a life force that
once flourished and even dreamed of grandeur.
But that was a long time ago, and what once thrived
now languishes, desperately needing a bailout, a break, a novena,
anything that would mend, brace, bind, or buy time.

The hours pass between them like a funeral procession.
She struggles to her feet, intent on administering some
form of leniency, but then withdraws from the room, her
intentions mute. The room has become a confessional and
forever will be, as she is forever a hostage to the confession.

Collaterally Damaged Conviction

We hear the sound of drumbeats coming from the east,
from Washington. We turn in that direction, and listen.
The beat quickens over the weeks and months, and grows fierce.
We hear the rattle of glass sabers raised high by insincere men.
Soon, armored columns form in a distant desert,
fighter jets split the skies, battleships arm their missiles,
and guns are greased by the millions.
It is time for war, they tell us.
It is only conviction that we lack.

Conviction demands a premium of resolve from the casual user.
It must be first-rate, steady, unerring, ruthlessly loyal,
and beyond question. It is the crusade of the moment
that feeds fear to the age of reason, a crusade that fails
to deliver its phantom expectations,
a crusade spun with intentions of hysteria.
The pennants of victory fly high before the first shot is fired.

A lazy assembly, carelessly maintained and easily distracted, is
seduced by the mesmerizing chants of electronic warriors
who press their faces against the windows of our brains,
and instruct us on our faultless duty to dismember and kill
those who would violate our mythology.

We consent.
Now, the battle-scorched wreckage of our mythology
is all that we have to bequeath to our children.

Conviction, collaterally damaged in the stampede of the crusade,
cowers behind the mushrooming vortex of the New Patriotism,
then retreats, sweet and melodic,
into the hushed delirium of contentment.

Dying as a Liar

I knew a liar once. Not just any liar, but a sensational one,
an antagonist, a puppeteer, a religionist devoted to the temple
of deceit. This was someone who practiced hard at his craft.
His every breath was spent in service to the lie, and to himself.

I bet you knew one, too.

He did not lack for skill. Cunning came by instinct.
All day long he worked, pontificating, manufacturing
truth to precise tolerances. Never mind the flaws under the
skin of his words, the parasites looking for an unsuspecting host,
or his dragons of deception. So long as it sounds polished,
lying will launch wars, fetch higher prices, and trick
a baby out of the arms of its mother.

Did you know that already?

It is curious that liars teach exemplary lessons of life.
Who wouldn't learn from a master? Every day was circus day,
the circus of the lie. When the missionaries were in town,
even they came to watch his acrobatics.
Watching was always at your own risk, as the liar vandalized
the good graces of his admirers.
And he slashed his skeptics using slander as his sword.

There is no sense in thinking too long about a lie if it
feels real. Like power, if a lie appears real, then it is. That's
what a liar will teach you.

But you knew that.

As with the sword, those who live by the lie,
die by the lie. In the end, the lie decays;
it cannot tolerate the test of scrutiny.
Neither can the liar.
In the end, the liar creates his own,
inevitable demise,
and dies as a liar,
alone, inglorious, and afraid.

Preacher and the Green Berets

When the silver-haired preacher regaled in the
airport terminal about the progress of the war,
he was contented, clutching a book on
God's response to the terrorist threat.

Flush from a week of Green Beret day camp for ministers,
the preacher told tales of power and might and
enviable virility.
He was persuaded that, in the name of an
affronted people of an affronted God,
violence is sanctified.

The enemy,
anonymous conscripts of our ogre du jour,
trapped and emaciated,
fell into the sands by the thousands,
vanquished by flights of foreign flame,
a wrath, divine and invincible, that consumed them
where they stood and where they wept, openly.

Where are all the sons, preacher?
Where are the fathers of the children?
And the brothers you are sworn to love?

They are assets that have been degraded, dear preacher.
This is what they tell us,
merely assets, of no concern to us.
The violence is sanitized.
Surely, at the end of the horrific siege,
you believe your savior to be pleased.

I absolve you, silver-haired preacher,
of unfettered glee
with the theater of soldiery.
But why your urgency to punish a heathen foe?
You cast adrift the commandments of compassion, and
as you locked the unlucky unbelievers steadily
in the cross hairs of damnation,
I wondered: Did they kneel before they died?

IV

Cascade Morning

In the early waking hours of the day, when the stars have
all but faded from the eastern sky, I look for the first flare
of light from the sun.

The usual cloak of clouds has fled, distracted by a weather
system approaching from the Pacific, or maybe from Canada.
Now the Cascade Mountains are soon to be revealed.
The mountains carve their signature silhouette against the
day's womb. Dawn appears jagged, the horizon broken.
Soon there will be an orange sky, accompanied by hues
of purple and pink.

With its hazy guardian gone, the Cascades must face the
audacity of the sun alone. Such uncontested access to the
mountains is rare, but not without precedent. The sun will not
squander this opportunity.

As it perfects its calculated assault, the sun rides to the top
of the spine of the elongated range, laughing as usual.
It rises higher and higher until at last,
day breaches the fortress of wood and stone,
and light flows sweetly, beatifically,
into the fawn of morning.

The Cascades, in resplendent surrender,
applaud.

Vanilla Strokes

This pen smells like vanilla.
Not that it meant to,
or if flavors were offered in a plebiscite,
would vote vanilla its first choice.

It got warehoused in an
otherwise unpretentious table drawer, deep enough
to become the official headquarters of vanilla candles.
A vanilla candle depot that never
seems to get retired, matches notwithstanding,
or go running off scentless into the night.

No, like loyal reservists,
the candle cadets perform their ancillary duties
(other duties as assigned)
like surreptitiously force-feeding my olfactory receptors.

Every time I raise my pen from where it slept,
I nibble on the black enamel as if it was
a dripping, voluptuous ice-cream cone
(do not try this at home).

I pray grapefruit candles do not go on sale tomorrow.

Shadow Face

For a Friday, this morning is rude.
It is the first day of summer, and the living room
is illuminated by the robust rays of a celebratory sun.

A momentary, perfect pitch of light, however,
reveals a secret, accidentally I am sure.
The accident framed in a square mirror reveals the
micro-shadows from hair-thin wrinkles in my mid-forties face
that are as benign as cub scouts, but in today's sun,
look like they've done hard time.

Until today, I was not a conspiracy theorist. Until today.
These wrinkles have been planned all along. This is facial
graffiti at its worst, and it shows evidence of gravity sailing
solo at night without a map, longitude and latitude be damned.

Or maybe gravity hired the services of a drunken navigator,
who drops anchor repeatedly at the bottoms of my cheekbones,
the corners of my eyes, the sphere of my forehead,
and, unappreciatively, the base of my belly
(another story for another time).

The lemon laws should be amended because time
sold me a warranty product, but by the looks of things today,
the warranty had a loophole from the beginning. The user fee
for the face doesn't kick in until the fifth decade. I have been
robbed of youth by the wiry shadows that now routinely
collect on my face like gangs of roosting ravens.

But I cannot deny the boxed and horror-filled face
that stares back at me while looking down at the
mirror in my hand.

The mirror tenders a summertime greeting:
Good morning—yes, you're old—now go to work!

Halloween Blind Date

At the withering insistence of Emma,
a hobbyist matchmaker of only the best intentions,
I agree to a blind date.

"She's a good, clean girl," Emma assures me.
She's from a good Asian family, I am told, sweet,
a fine personality,
a doctor, successful pathologist,
a fair English-as-a-second-language student,
but otherwise a good biography.

The awkward dinner-table talk begins with
an obligatory team cheer for our intrepid Emma.
Then the distance between words begins to grow,
our accents thicken, and the subject matter shrivels.

We begin to talk about work, the universal default topic.
What better topic on Halloween than autopsies?

"How do you deal with the maggots?"
"Oh, it's really no problem," she says, "I just work
around them. Except when they begin to crawl up my sleeve.
Then I must stop and flick them off."
Enchanting.

The match-made date is not only blind,
it is pathologically dead (but who will tell Emma?).
The slow art of eating defers to the
urgency of a merciful closure to our most delicate date.

After an honorable escort to her apartment door,
I pause awkwardly before stepping inside for a moment.
We nervously stumble over accents a few more times,
then we lie about getting together again sometime, and I
make a clean escape. Perhaps, by next Halloween, Emma will
perfect her happy hobby.

Orchids at the Royal Kew Gardens

Strolling through the orchid collection at the Royal Botanical
Kew Gardens is like walking through a parade of prisms.
There are purple and pale yellow, lavender and pink, blue, red,
chocolate brown and white cream, lime and orange.

It's enough to drive you to the cafeteria. Or you can stay and
focus on the lips of the enticing petals parted wide like a star or
a spider. It seems they are prepared, depending on your fortune,
to deliver a kiss or a swift bite.

Some orchids drip like a necklace from a mossy field
in a tree trunk. They cling nonchalantly to the knotty wood,
where they are nestled, gem by delicious gem,
into nature's perfectly planned crevices.

The disparate colors collide with the imagination of your eyes
and stream like a comet's glittering tail through the
Princess of Wales Conservatory. Copper Wing, Gypsy Queen,
and Happy Girl are but a few of the ringleaders
strategically arranged to command your attention.

Look and you will see that they have freckles, that
they are tigers and moons and bursts of fireworks.
Look closer and you will visit Costa Rica, Madagascar,
New Guinea, Borneo, and Africa.
Look too closely and you will feel like you just
took a Rorschach test.

The maniacal botanical proclivities of the British
can never be underestimated.
Who else feeds an army of five thousand species of one plant?
"Relax your gaze at your own risk" is a sign they should post
everywhere. The kaleidoscope of an over-achieving orchid
collection stuns consciousness and arrests any recollection of,
or remote interest in, other photosynthetic members of the
united plant kingdom.

Unsuspecting onlookers approach for an intimate experience with the smiling sirens cleverly disguised as innocent flowers sent out for a boring tan. We, the poor patrons, succumb to the visual nectar of seduction and linger to drink it in, never to be seen sensible again.

God save the Queen, and the rest of us.

Mailing Moonlight

When I opened my mailbox tonight,
it was filled with moonlight.

Not a lethargic light,
but a silky fire that sliced past the opened lid,
bounced recklessly against the plain grainy tin walls, and
landed with a thud when it shimmied up to the unwelcome
bill left by our absent-minded postman
(might it have been a light bill?).
Would he believe me if I told him that he delivered
moonlight this time around?

Just as I pondered that very thought,
I felt someone grinning over my shoulder.
I turned and looked.
There it was,
the moon, loitering in the sky,
gloating at its mischievous deed.

Enamored with the immensity of its presence,
the moon betrayed a hint of surprise that
a humble green miniature barn of a mailbox,
with its reliable red flag,
could so comfortably conceal a piece of lunar light
that cleverly slipped inside and
entertained a day's worth of uncollected mail.

On Tuesday

The ironing chore falls behind before I can get started.
Rosie, the bespectacled old lady across the street, serves up a
cup of transparent coffee.
She is glad for the early morning visit
before her solitary assault on the day's jigsaw puzzle.

Back home, upstairs, my hands are wrapped around
a cup of coffee, poured hot and dark as a silhouette.
I notice out my window that my transient February friend has
laid claim to a fork of the cedar tree, nesting in a bed
of twigs skillfully assembled and meticulously maintained.

The raccoon yawns through the lull of the cold,
damp morning air. He rolls on his back and arches his
front paws up and over his head. He coils tightly to avoid the
face of frost that grows ever-longer teeth as noon slips into the
infancy of evening. Soon, hidden nocturnal jewels will serve as
trophies for his tongue.

Without warning, a mob of clouds gathers and gestures
threats of a deluge.
But the threats prove idle, and the mob, impotent,
disperses peacefully, but not without hurling a few
insults and marking the air with the scent of menace.

To me, and to the sleeping bandit in the tree,
rolled into a striped sphere of fur,
they are irrelevant this Tuesday.

River Pilot

From the steady passage of an anonymous ship,
the wake is dispatched like a messenger to the
shores of Astoria.
Subdued and silent, the wake
delivers its signal—the ship is ready.

A practiced drill unfolds with this ship,
as with the one before it, and the one to follow.
An intrepid pilot boat spirits a river pilot through the
successive walls of rain, and against the
concussions of the Columbia River's agitated waves.
The ship slows for the anticipated rendezvous.

A determined climb up the steel ladder,
and the pilot is secure,
while another pilot, fresh from threading the ship
through the labyrinth of the sand
convulsing in the river's mouth,
climbs down the salt-pocked ladder onto the deck of
the obliging pilot boat. The captain speeds the pilot
to shore, and the pilot waits for the next passage of a ship.

It is small drama, a fleeting glimpse of
the one later in the night, and tomorrow.
You imagine what the pilot thinks about in the driving rain,
in the middle of the night, in below-freezing weather,
when he finds himself climbing a ladder suspended
above ferocious waters that would surely drag him into
the abyss should he miss a rung or catch a sudden gust of wind.

If he had taken the draftsman job, he would be
home now, sitting by the fireplace, cradling his daughter, and
reading out loud about a goose, or a captive princess, or
a bunch of bears that left their house unlocked.

But then again, he wonders, how often do you get to take a
river for a lover.

Safely aboard the ship, the river pilot resumes speed,
and plies the gray, gifting waters of the Columbia,
praying to slip through to his destination, unmolested.

Fallibility

As orphans go, fallibility is criminally overlooked.
It abandons pretenses without a fight,
in favor of full disclosure of its intentions, but not its timing.
It embraces diversity and invites adversity.
Optimists are its favorite food—zealots for dessert.
But for holidays and special occasions, megalomaniacs
are the entree.

Self-defense is not necessarily futile. A well-planned calendar
should be a weapon of choice. Fallibility excels as a field
marshal with an impeccable sense of attack. The endearments
of fallibility yield unimaginably good fortune, usually for
someone else.

But fallibility is also a compassionate teacher who dotes
on us. Surrendering to this reality now spares us the misery
of protracted disappointment and ill-humored humiliation.
Good students, like loyal soldiers, should take note, salute,
and go about their daily idiosyncrasies.

Gayle's Sugar-White Pergola

The intertwining arms of the sugar-white pergola cut graphite
shadows across the horizontal layers of our house's sage-green
wall. Compliant shadows, under strict orders from the sun,
twist discreetly, minute by beckoning minute,
as the sun drifts west to the next haphazardly drawn time zone,
and the jagged one after that.

But shadow-craft is only volunteer duty for the pergola.
Its principal purpose is to frame the turquoise of the sky,
box the shifting wrinkles in the clouds, and
tickle the ribs of the wind until it laughs in baritones through
deep-throated chimes suspended from the center.

Its creator stakes proud claim in the ground that the earth can
and must be adorned in a red-brick bordered, cookie-cut back
yard, with its façade cottage garage and off-center birdhouse on
the southern fence.

The clay medallion clock on the wall says it is time for the sun
to be excused and for the paint blisters to take refuge in the
cool of the night, when the pyramid crowns of the sugar-white
pergola strain to reach up and ply the passing seas of
floating stars and lounging planets. Or invite, on behalf of the
pergola proper, the first rainy waves of a Pacific storm that will,
no doubt, overstay its ambivalent welcome.

Rainy Day Dog

Nikki cocks her head up, ears at peak attention.
The rain pinpricks against the vast plate of a
double-paned window.
The wind is announcing winter, again.
A nervous rotation of the left ear, now the right.
She takes another studied glance out at the canvas
of the window, then the door, and then checks in with me.
The false alarm is duly noted,
and her head slowly drops back down
to the warm and worn cotton blanket
on the paw-plucked chaise lounge.
An eyebrow arches—just one—as
the obliging eyes perform a final security sweep.
It's only rain…just rain.
Goodnight again, girl.
Now, go catch a dream by the tail.

Ruby Dusk

El Paso scorns my absence, but I do not care.
A detour will delay my return from Washington, D.C.
Instead, I am implored to travel to the other Washington,
and to Seattle.
I cannot refuse.

In Seattle, I am a novice Northwest explorer.
I look up from the tarmac to see a blanketed sky.
The clouds and the tarmac are the same color.
It is a bizarre sight for a dweller of the desert, where the
sun punishes clouds that dare cast a shadow.

Yakima is the next stop, the last stop on this long day.
The propeller-driven plane climbs into the air with the
enthusiasm of a yawn, advancing eastward, in no
particular hurry, just under the bubbled skirt of the
murky ceiling.

It is gray out my window. All the world is gray and getting dark
and depressing. Suddenly, with a burst of bravado, the pilot
arches plane and passengers upward, and punches through an
eye in the face of the corrugated clouds. Above the celestial veil
there is the snowy peak of a monolith.

An ancient temple of worship,
she has come to be known as Rainier, so christened by
the white man. The canopy of gray beneath us is soon
transformed into a flaming sea of crimson, departing
compliments of a setting sun.
It is as if God has broken open a ruby
and poured it out over the clouds.
And into the heart of a grateful traveler.

Glossary of Spanish Words

conquista. Conquest; the Spanish conquest of the New World.

coyotes. In the vernacular of the United States-Mexico border region, smugglers of human cargo.

hermano. Brother.

Norteamérica. North America. In Mexico, the United States is commonly referred to as Norteamérica.

pistolero. Gunman.

vieja. Old lady, wife.